I0006590

New ABAP Language features in ABAP 7.4 and 7.5

By Mark Anderson

Contents

New ABAP 7.4 and 7.5 Language Features

With the release of ABAP 7.4 and 7.5 several new ABAP language features have been introduced. These new language statements improve the existing ABAP syntax and adds new language capabilities.

These are easy to use and reduces the number of lines we need to code to achieve the same functionality. The new language features have been added without taking away the old syntax (ensuring backward compatibility).

1. New Language Features

1.1   Inline Declarations

It had always been considered as a practice in SAP to declare the variables at the beginning of the program. But most developers ended up declaring the variables, just before using it. With inline declarations SAP has made this practice acceptable and the preferred way of declaration.

Inline declarations are a new way of declaring variables and field symbols. This enables the programmers to declare the variable at the time when they are required, as opposed to declaring it at the start of the program.

The data type of most of the variables are knows as they are either changing parameters of a procedure or the values are assigned from an existing variable. Hence, the compiler knows what to check against. Thus, with the new language statements it makes sense to let the compiler derive the type of the new variables without having to declare it explicitly.

Let us look at the below example where we want to assign a value to the variable:

Example 1: Assign value to a variable

Before release 7.40

```
DATA l_str_val TYPE string.
l_str_val = 'Hello World'.
```

With release 7.40

```
DATA(l_str_val) = 'Hello World'.
```

With the above new feature, the complier already knows that it can and needs to store the value of 'Hello World' in a String variable. Hence, there is no explicit need to declare a variable of type String.

The above code does not only reduce the number of lines but is also easier to understand.

Let us look at another example where we have to loop over an internal table and assign a value to the work area.

Example 2: Loop over an internal table

Before release 7.40

```
DATA l_wa LIKE LINE OF i_tab.
LOOP AT i_tab INTO l_wa.
    ...
ENDLOOP.
```

With release 7.40

```
LOOP AT i_tab INTO DATA (l_wa).
    ...
ENDLOOP.
```

Every time we need to loop over an internal table we need to declare a work area. Many a times this work area is also not of any use once the loop processing is complete.

Hence with inline declarations it makes it easy to declare it and use when it is required.

Below are some more examples of inline declarations:

Example 3: Loop over internal table and assign it to a field symbol

Before release 7.40

```
FIELD-SYMBOLS: <f_line> TYPE ....

LOOP AT i_tab ASSIGNING <f_line>.
 ...
ENDLOOP.
```

With release 7.40

```
LOOP AT i_tab ASSIGNING FIELD-
SYMBOL(<f_line>).
 ...
ENDLOOP.
```

This is similar to Example 2, except that it uses Field symbols instead of work area.

Example 4: Read a line of internal table and assign it to a field symbol

Before release 7.40

```
FIELD-SYMBOLS: <line> TYPE ....

READ TABLE i_tab ASSIGNING <line>.
```

With release 7.40

```
READ TABLE i_tab ASSIGNING FIELD-
SYMBOL(<line>).
```

Example 5: Select from database into an internal table

Before release 7.40

```
DATA: i_tab TYPE TABLE OF dtab.
```

```
SELECT * FROM dtab
      INTO TABLE i_tab
      WHERE fld = lv_fld.
```

With release 7.40

```
SELECT * FROM dtab
INTO TABLE @DATA(i_tab)
WHERE fld = @lv_fld.
```

You would have noticed that you would have to put @ symbol in front of your variables (or constants) used in select statements when using the new features. This helps the complier in understanding that we are not referring to the fields in the database but variables in the program.

Example 5: Select specific fields from database into an internal table

Before release 7.40

```
SELECT SINGLE field1 field2
    FROM dbtab
    INTO  (lv_field1 , lv_field2)
    WHERE ...

    WRITE: / lv_field1, lv_field2.
```

With release 7.40

```
SELECT SINGLE field1 AS fld1,
              field2 AS fld2
        FROM dbtab
        INTO @DATA(ls_structure)
        WHERE ...

WRITE: / ls_structure-fld1, ls_structure-
fld2
```

Please note that when using new features, you also must put commas between the fields you are retrieving from the database and put the INTO statement at the end.

1.2 Internal Tables

In previous section we saw that it was possible to read the internal table into a work area without having to declare the work area before the read statement. This change would remove extra data declaration lines.

However, if you adopt the new features completely, you might never have to use the read statement.

Below are some examples:

Example 1: Reading a row from an internal table using index

Before release 7.40

```
READ TABLE i_tab INDEX idx
        INTO wa.
```

With release 7.40

```
wa = i_tab[ idx ].
```

Example 2: Assign value to a variable

Before release 7.40

```
READ TABLE i_tab INDEX idx
        USING KEY key
        INTO wa.
```

With release 7.40

```
wa = i_tab[ KEY key INDEX idx ].
```

Example 3: Reading a table with key

Before release 7.40

```
READ TABLE i_tab
        WITH KEY col1 = …
```

```
                col2 = ...
        INTO wa.
```

With release 7.40

```
    wa = i_tab[ col1 = ... col2 = ... ].
```

Example 4: Check if a line exists

Before release 7.40

```
        READ TABLE i_tab ...
            TRANSPORTING NO FIELDS.
        IF sy-subrc = 0.
          ...
        ENDIF.
```

With release 7.40

```
        IF line_exists( i_tab[ ... ] ).
        ...
        ENDIF.
```

Example 5: Get table index

Before release 7.40

```
        DATA i_dx type sy-tabix.
        READ TABLE ...
           TRANSPORTING NO FIELDS.
          I_dx = sy-tabix.
```

With release 7.40

```
        DATA(i_dx) =
                line_index( i_tab[ ... ] ).
```

The above new language features come with a catch that if the value
is not found then an exception (CX_SY_ITAB_LINE_NOT_FOUND) is

raised and if the exception is not caught then there will be a short dump.

Therefore, SAP recommends that the value should be assigned to a field symbol and then we could check the value using sy-subrc.

```
ASSIGN l_tab[ 1 ] to FIELD-SYMBOL(<ls_tab>).
IF sy-subrc = 0.

ENDIF.
```

1.3   String Processing

String processing is very frequently used in ABAP code. The data from the database often needs to be formatted before it is displayed to the user and vice versa. E.g. if we have to display the sales order details on the screen, then we might have to concatenate a text with the Sales order number and then display it.

Following are some instances where string processing are required:

- Convert Input data before using it in Database operations

- Convert data from data base into a more human readable form.

1.3.1 Concatenation of strings

Concatenation is simplified in ABAP 7.4. In some cases, they replace the old way of concatenating and in other cases they also introduce new functionality.

Below are some important changes:

- String Templates: the option to create a character string out of literal texts, expressions, and control characters.

- Chaining Operator: chain two character-like operands into one new character string.

- Character String Functions: built-in functions for searching, processing and comparing strings.

CONCATENATE prior to ABAP 7.4

One of the common uses of concatenate statement is to display the data in a more human readable form.
Let us take an example where you need to show the Sales order number to the user. Just displaying the order number in the screen might not be the best. Hence, you might be required to concatenate some literals.

```
DATA: lv_order TYPE string,
      lv_out   TYPE string.

lv_order = l_vbak-vbeln.


CONCATENATE 'Your Sales order number is:'
            lv_order
            INTO lv_out
            SEPARATED BY space.

WRITE:/ lv_out.
```

```
Your Sales order number is: 0000005723
```

CONCATENATE ABAP 7.4

```
DATA: lv_order TYPE string,
      lv_out   TYPE string.

lv_order = l_vbak-vbeln.

lv_out = |Your Sales order number is:| && lv_order
         .

WRITE:/ lv_out.
```

```
Your Sales order number is: 0000005723
```

As you would have noticed, ABAP now has a new concatenation operator, &&.

String Templates

The purpose of a string template is to create a new character string out of literal texts and embedded expressions. It largely replaces the use of the WRITE TO statement.

A string template is defined by using the | (pipe) symbol at the beginning and end of a template.

```
DATA: character_string TYPE string.
character_string = |This is a literal text.|.
```

This example has in fact the same result as:

```
character_string = `This is a literal text.`.
```

The added value of a string template becomes clear when combining literal texts with embedded expressions and control characters. Embedded expressions are defined within a string template with curly brackets { expression }. Note that a space between bracket and expression is obligatory.

An expression can be a data object (variable), a functional method, a predefined function or a calculation expression. Some examples are:

```
character_string = |{ a_numeric_variable }|.

character_string = |This resulted in return code {
sy-subrc }|.

character_string = |The length of text element 001
({ text-001 }) is { strlen(text-001 ) }|.
```

Embedded expressions have a default output format, but also several formatting options, comparable to the format options of the WRITE statement.

Example:

```
DATA: comm_capital    TYPE bzusage VALUE '1234567.1
23',
      currency_field TYPE swhr,
      lv_string      TYPE string.


lv_string = |{ comm_capital CURRENCY = currency_fi
eld  NUMBER = USER }|.
```

The above code snippet converts the amount in a display format as per user settings.

The value of the amount is assigned in the declaration as '1234567.123'.

This is converted into '1.234.567,12' after the String operation.

Chaining Operator

The Chaining Operator && can be used to create one-character string out of multiple other strings and string templates.

In this example, a number text, a space, an existing character string and a new string template are concatenated into a new character string.

```
character_string   =   'Text literal'(002) && ` ` &&
character_string && |{
amount_field NUMBER = USER }|.
```

1.3.2 ALPHA Formatting

Formatting functions CONVERSION_EXIT_ALPHA_INPUT and CONVERSION_EXIT_ALPHA_OUTPUT is used very frequently to add and remove leading zeroes from data. It adds to the number of lines of code but does not provide much business logic. E.g. it might be required to remove the zeroes when showing messages to the user, but then add them back before you read the database.

Remove leading zeroes before output to user

```
l_ordernum = '0000012345'.

CALL FUNCTION 'CONVERSION_EXIT_ALPHA_OUTPUT'
   EXPORTING
      input          = l_ordernum
   IMPORTING
      OUTPUT         = l_ordernum.
```

Add leading zeroes back before database read

```
l_ordernum = '12345'.

CALL FUNCTION 'CONVERSION_EXIT_ALPHA_INPUT'
   EXPORTING
      input          = l_ordernum
   IMPORTING
      OUTPUT         = l_ordernum.
```

The above can be done in a much simpler manner.

Remove Leading zeros

```
DATA(lv_vbeln) = '0000012345'.
lv_vbeln = / |{ lv_vbeln  ALPHA = OUT }|.
```

Add leading zeros

```
DATA(lv_vbeln) = '12345'.
lv_vbeln = |{ lv_vbeln  ALPHA = IN }|.
```

1.4   Calling functions

1.4.1 Method chaining

During the processing of a Class method or a Function module you will need to execute more granular Function modules, Class methods, form routines etc.

Many a times, the values returned from one call needs to be passed as an input to the next call. Hence the developer ends up creating temporary variables. These variables do not add any value but are just used in receiving data from one call and passing it to the next call.

With ABAP 7.02, SAP introduced Method chaining. With this, the user could pass the values without the use of temporary variables.

Let us look at the below example of old way of coding.

e.g. we need to get the email id of the business partner and then pass it to the email service. This would require getting the email and store it in the local variable. Then this value would be passed to the email method.

```
l_bp_emailid = lo_bp->get_email( i_bp = l_bp ).
lo_email->send_email( l_bp_emailid ).
```

With Method chaining you can achieve the same results as follows:

```
lo_email->send_email( lo_bp-
>get_email( i_bp = l_bp  ).
```

1.4.2 Avoiding type mismatch dumps when calling functions

ABAPers are familiar with the Type Mismatch dump which happens if the type of the variable does not match with the parameter definition of the Function Modules. With a method, you get a syntax error; with a function module, you get a short dump at runtime. The process of checking the data types of the parameters, declaring the variables and resolving these dumps are quite tedious and not required.

Since the compiler already knows which types are expected, it would be best to allow the compiler to decide the data type.

e.g.

```
CALL METHOD lo_bus_partner->update_address(
   EXPORTING
      i_address   = wa_address
   IMPORTING
      e_message       = DATA(lo_message)

   ).
```

As you can see from the above example the variable for the message was not declared with a DATA statement.

1.5   CONVersion Operator

Conversion operator converts a value into a specified type. It is suitable for avoiding the declaration of helper variables.

For Example, let us assume that a method expects a string, but you have the data in a text field. As per the old syntax you would need to move the value to a string variable and then pass this helper variable to the method call. With CONV operator the helper variable is no more required.

Before release 7.40

```
DATA cust_name TYPE c LENGTH 20.
DATA helper TYPE string.

helper = cust_name.

cl_func=>process_func( i_name = helper ).
```

In the above code snippet, cust_name is a character of length 20. But the method process_function expects a string. Hence in the old syntax it was required to move the data to a variable which was type compatible with the method parameters.

With release 7.40

```
DATA cust_name TYPE c LENGTH 20.

cl_func=>process_func( i_name = CONV string( cust_
name ) ).
```

In such cases it is even simpler to write

```
DATA cust_name TYPE c LENGTH 20.

cl_func=>process_func( i_name = CONV #( cust_name
) ).
```

With the new syntax, the helper variable (helper) is not required. The value can be converted directly during the method call.

The syntax of the CONV operator is as follows:

```
... CONV dtype|#( ... ) ...
```

If the value of the type can be derived (as in our example) then the data type ('dtype') is not required. It is sufficient to use the '#'.

1.6   CASTing Operator

The casting operator CAST is a constructor operator that performs a down cast or an up cast for the argument object and creates a reference variable as a result.

The syntax of the CASTing operator is as follows:

```
... CAST #/type( [let_exp] dobj ) ...
```

The 'type' can be specified as:

- Class or an Interface.

- The '#' character is a symbol for the operand 'type'. This can be used only when the operand type is unique and fully identifiable.
- any non-generic data type dtype or the fully generic data type data

Example of Down Cast

Let us assume that you need all the components of a structure. This is done by getting the metadata of the structure by calling method CL_ABAP_STRUCTDESCR=> DESCRIBE_BY_NAME. This returns a reference to description object TYPE REF TO CL_ABAP_TYPEDESCR. The returned reference can be used to get the components of the structure.

Before release 7.40

```
DATA structdescr TYPE REF TO cl_abap_structdescr.

structdescr ?= cl_abap_typedescr=>describe_by_name
( 'ZBP_STRUCT' ).

DATA components   TYPE abap_compdescr_tab.

components = structdescr->components.
```

In the above code we first get the details of the structure in a helper variable structdescr and then use this to get the components.

With release 7.40

```
DATA(components) = CAST cl_abap_structdescr(
   cl_abap_typedescr=>describe_by_name( 'ZBP_STRUCT' ) )-
>components.
```

With the new syntax you do not need the helper variable structdescr.

1.7   VALUE Operator

The value operator VALUE is a constructor operator that creates a value for the type specified with 'type'.

You could construct an initial value for any data type.

Example 1: Create an internal table and fill it with initial values as shown below:

```
TYPES char_tab TYPE TABLE OF char20 WITH EMPTY KEY
.

DATA(chardata) = VALUE char_tab( ( 'Firstrow' ) (
'Secondrow' ) ( 'Thirdrow' ) ).
```

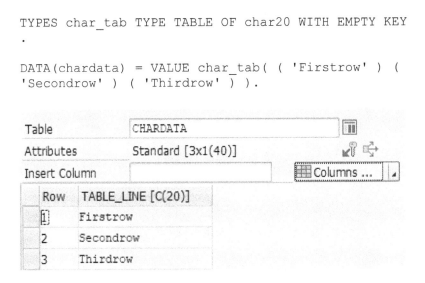

Example 2: Create an internal table, where for each line a value can be assigned.

```
TYPES: BEGIN OF t_struct,
          col1 TYPE char10,
          col2 TYPE char10,
        END OF t_struct.

DATA itab TYPE TABLE OF t_struct.

itab = VALUE #( ( col1 = 'Col1Row1' col2 = 'Col2Ro
w1' )
```

```
                              ( col1 = 'Col1Row2' col2 = 'Col2Ro
   w2' ) ).
```

Table	ITAB	
Attributes	Standard [2x2(40)]	
Insert Column		Columns ...

Row	COL1 [C(10)]	COL2 [C(10)]
1	Col1Row1	Col2Row1
2	Col1Row2	Col2Row2

Example 3: Construct a ranges table and fills it with four rows while using the short form for structured row types.

```
DATA itab TYPE RANGE OF i.

itab = VALUE #( sign = 'I'  option = 'BT' ( low =
1   high = 10 )
                                      ( low =
21 high = 30 )
                                      ( low =
41 high = 50 )
                         option = 'GE' ( low =
61 )  ).
```

Table	ITAB	
Attributes	Standard [4x4(16)]	
Insert Column		Columns ...

Row	SIGN [C(1)]	OPTION [C(2)]	LOW [I(4)]	HIGH [I(4)]
1	I	BT	1	10
2	I	BT	21	30
3	I	BT	41	50
4	I	GE	61	0

Note that you cannot construct elementary values (which is possible with instantiation operator NEW) – simply because there is no need for it.

1.8   FOR operator

FOR operator is used to loop at an internal table. For each loop the row is read and assigned to a Work area or a field symbol. This is similar to the FOR loop we would have used in C language.

Example 1: Transfer our data from one internal table to another

Before 7.4 we had to loop over the first table, assign the value to the work area of the new table and then append the work area into the new table.
e.g.

```
LOOP AT lt_sales ASSIGNING FIELD-
SYMBOL(<fs_sales>).

  lv_sales_no = <fs_sales>-vbeln.

  APPEND lv_sales_no TO lt_all_sales.

  CLEAR : lv_sales_no.

ENDLOOP.
```

In the new syntax the above operation can be done as shown below:

```
DATA(lt_all_sales)
= VALUE tt_sales( FOR ls_sales IN lt_sales ( ls_sa
les-vbeln ) ).
```

Example 2: For with Where condition

```
TYPES:
  BEGIN OF ty_business_partner,
    partner TYPE char10,
```

```
    name      TYPE char30,
    city      TYPE char30,
    route     TYPE char10,
  END    OF ty_business_partner.

TYPES: tt_bus_partner TYPE SORTED TABLE OF ty_business_p
artner
         WITH UNIQUE KEY partner.

TYPES: tt_citys TYPE STANDARD TABLE OF char30 WITH EMPTY
 KEY.

DATA(t_BP) =
  VALUE tt_bus_partner(
    ( partner = 'BP0001' name = 'PeterParker' city = 'NY
'  route = 'R0001' )
    ( partner = 'BP0002' name = 'Superman'    city = 'LA
'  route = 'R0003' )
    ( partner = 'BP0003' name = 'Batman'      city = 'DF
W' route = 'R0001' )
    ( partner = 'BP0004' name = 'IronMan'     city = 'CH
'  route = 'R0003' )
  ).

* FOR to get the column CITY
DATA(t_city) =
  VALUE tt_citys( FOR ls_bp IN t_BP WHERE ( route = 'R00
01' ) ( ls_bp-city ) ).
```

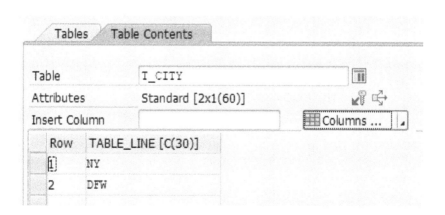

1.9   Reduction operator REDUCE

Reduce operator creates a result of specified data type after going through iterations. In classical ABAP if we had to evaluate the data in an internal table then we had to loop through the internal table, evaluate the condition and then take appropriate action. This could be done in a much simpler way with Reduce.

Syntax:

```
... REDUCE type(
INIT result = start_value
    ...
FOR for_exp1
FOR for_exp2
...
NEXT ...
        result = iterated_value
... )
```

Example 1: Count lines of table that meet a condition (field city contains "LA").

```
TYPES:
  BEGIN OF ty_business_partner,
    partner   TYPE char10,
    name      TYPE char30,
    city      TYPE char30,
    route     TYPE char10,
  END   OF ty_business_partner.

TYPES: tt_bus_partner TYPE SORTED TABLE OF ty_business_p
artner
          WITH UNIQUE KEY partner.

DATA(t_BP) =
  VALUE tt_bus_partner(
    ( partner = 'BP0001' name = 'PeterParker' city = 'NY
'    route = 'R0001' )
    ( partner = 'BP0002' name = 'Superman'    city = 'LA
'    route = 'R0003' )
    ( partner = 'BP0003' name = 'Batman'      city = 'DF
W'   route = 'R0001' )
    ( partner = 'BP0004' name = 'IronMan'     city = 'LA
'    route = 'R0003' )
```

```
).
```

```
" Before 7.40
DATA: lv_lines TYPE i.
LOOP AT t_bp INTO DATA(ls_bp) WHERE city = 'LA'.
  lv_lines = lv_lines + 1.
ENDLOOP.
```

With the new syntax it is not required to loop through all the records to count the number of matches.

The REDUCE operator can be used instead

```
DATA(lv_lines) = REDUCE i( INIT x = 0 FOR wa_bp IN t_BP
                    WHERE ( city = 'LA' ) NEXT x = x + 1
  ).
```

1.10 Conditional operators COND

It is an excepted practice in ABAP to use CASE statements instead of IF statement. CASE statements made the code readable but had an issue that it was not able to evaluate multiple conditions.

Hence in many instances, the ABAPers had to move back to using IF..ELSE..ENDIF constructs. Let us look at the below example:

```
DATA: lv_text(30).

IF lv_prod_catg = '10' AND lv_prodtype = 'A'.
    lv_text = 'Television'.
ELSE.
IF lv_prod_catg ='20' AND lv_prodtype = 'B'.
   lv_text = 'Automatic Washing Machine'
ELSE.
IF lv_prod_catg ='20' AND lv_prodtype = 'C'.
    lv_text = 'Semi-Automatic Washing Machine'.


   ..
ENDIF.
```

The above conditions are not possible by using Case statements as the WHEN clause could only evaluate either the lv_prod_catg or the lv_prodtype. This is where the new COND operator comes handy. COND allows us to evaluate multiple variables.

Syntax:

```
... COND dtype|#( WHEN log_exp1 THEN result1
                [ WHEN log_exp2 THEN result2 ]
                ...
                [ ELSE resultn ] ) ...
```

Example 1:

```
TRY.
 DATA(lv_text) =
          COND #( WHEN lv_prod_catg = '10' AND
lv_prodtype = 'A'
                            THEN 'Television'
                WHEN lv_prod_catg ='20' AND lv_prodtype
 = 'B'
                            THEN 'Automatic Washing
 Machine'
                WHEN lv_prod_catg ='20' AND lv_prodtype
 = 'C'
                            THEN 'Semi-Automatic Washing
 Machine'
                ELSE THROW  cx_exception( ) ).
   CATCH cx_exception.
 ENDTRY.
```

1.11 Conditional operators SWITCH

SWITCH is a conditional operator like CASE but more powerful and with much less coding.

It is used to switch from one value to another, based on a condition.

Syntax:

```
... SWITCH dtype|#( operand
                    WHEN const1 THEN result1
                  [ WHEN const2 THEN result2 ]
                    ...
                  [ ELSE resultn ] ) ...
```

Example 1:

```
DATA(lv_status) = SWITCH #( lv_flag
                            WHEN 'X' THEN
'Completed'
                            ELSE 'In Process'
                   ).
```

In the above example based on the value of the flag the value of the status is assigned to the lb_status variable.

1.12 Corresponding Operator

This operator allows the copy of data from one internal table to another internal table (just like move-corresponding) but provides more options on which columns are copied. With this new statement it is possible to not copy the values of one column even it the same column exists in the target internal table. It is also possible to copy data between columns which have different names in the source and target internal tables.

Syntax:

```
... CORRESPONDING type ( [BASE ( base )] struct|itab
[mapping|except] )
```

Example:

Workareas contains the following data:

```
L_workarea1 = VALUE line1 ( col1 = 1 col2 = 2 ).

L_workarea2
= VALUE line2 ( col1 = 4 col2 = 5 col3 = 6 ).
```

Example 1: The contents of L_Workarea1 are moved to L_Workarea2 where there is a matching column name. Where there is no match the column of L_Workarea2 is initialized.

```
L_workarea2 = CORRESPONDING # (L_workarea1).
```

Now the contents of the L_Workarea2 will have the following data:

```
L_workarea2 = ( col1 = 1 col2 = 2 col3 = 0 ).
```

Example 2: This uses the existing contents of L_workarea2 as a base and overwrites the matching columns from ls_line1.

This is exactly like MOVE-CORRESPONDING.

```
L_workarea2 = CORRESPONDING
# ( BASE ( L_workarea2) L_workarea1 ).
```

Now the contents of the Workarea2 will have the following data:

```
L_workarea2 = ( col1 = 1 col2 = 2 col3 = 6 ).
```

In this example L_workarea2 is used as a based. This means that the contents of L_workarea2 cannot be overwritten. All other fields take the value from L_workarea1.

Example 3: This creates a third and new structure (ls_line3) which is based on ls_line2 but overwritten by matching columns of ls_line1

```
    DATA(ls_line3) = CORRESPONDING line2( BASE (
ls_line2 ) ls_line1 ).
```

The contents of the Workarea3 will have the following data:

```
    L_workarea3 =( col1 = 1 col2 = 2 col3 = 6 ).
```

Example 3 has the same result as Example 2, but in Example 3 the data is populated into a new structure L_workarea3.

2. Summary

This book covered some of the important and frequently used new language features. This is only meant as a starting point for the more inquisitee developer and should be explored further. As mentioned earlier the new language features not only simply the code and reduces the number of lines but is also easier to understand.

www.ingramcontent.com/pod-product-compliance
Lightning Source LLC
Chambersburg PA
CBHW080606060326
40689CB00021B/4948